D1528530

MOTHER

TRUTHS

MOTHER TRUTHS

Poems on early
motherhood

Karen McMillan

For Casey
In becoming a mother,
I lost my mind a bit.
But found my voice.
And more importantly, you.
Love you forever.

CONTENTS

HOW DO I TELL YOU?

Future mum
I want to hold you
Super tight

I want to give a little warning
Without giving you a fright

The trials that you face
Flash before my eyes

Then I remember
This is your journey
Not mine

Besides
How do I really describe
The Good
The Bad
And the *Love*?

How do I tell you that
The seas are kind of rough?

How do I explain that
You'll forever be enough?

Because it's not like the adverts
It's not like they said

It's better in some ways
But just not how you expect

There's beauty to be found
In all the change
And the mess

In that strange sacred space
Between new beginnings and the end

I want to tell the truth
Without filling your head

I want to speak the things
That will stand you in good stead

I want to get real
Without igniting dread

So I took pen to paper
And wrote this book instead

THE THINGS YOU'LL MISS

Oh, nothing can prepare you
For having a child
They say, rather helpfully
With a knowing smile

But I think we can do
Better than that
By sharing the good
But also the bad

Let's at least try
To describe
What it really feels like
So they can glimpse the whole apple
Before taking a bite

So, expectant friend
Here's my little gift to you
A look at the things we miss most
Or, at least, I do

A bucket list, if you like
Of the things to really savour
So you can squeeze them in now
Then maybe thank me later

Slowly enjoy breakfast
Without the ensuing food-fight
Then stay in the bath
Until you're all prune-like

Washing your face
At a leisurely pace
The whole works:
Cleansing, toning, exfoliation

Then out the house when you want
Without the 45 minute
Prep situation

Uninterrupted chats
With your sister on the phone
Without *be careful,*
please get down
or *leave that alone*

Preparing long-winded recipes
To suit your own taste
Cooking with both hands
Personal space

Weekends spent watching all the TV
Loud inappropriate music
Instead of the *Wiggles* and *Blippi*

Being outside the house gone seven-thirty
Impromptu late-night food shopping
Spontaneity!

Getting in late
Flopping straight into bed
Oh just leave the dishes
We'll do them tomorrow instead

And my most pertinent
Piece of advice for you?
For God's sake
Savour that solo poo

NO SIGN YET?

I've never been so popular
My phone's been ringing off the hook
Maybe they don't believe me
Perhaps they'd like to take a look

At my cervix
Is it dilating?
No?
Well, I'm so sorry to keep you waiting

And that random girl from school
Who I've not spoken to in years
Well, of course *you'll* be
The first to know
When the babies head appears

As I waddle down the street
Looking several shades of rough
I'm commandeered
By strangers here
Getting handsy with my bump

That baby not arrived yet?
You must be totally fed up

Nope. Not yet
Funnily enough
That's why I look
So totally
Still very much
Up the duff

Get yourself a nice vindaloo
Washed down with some raspberry tea
Then one last night of passion
That did the trick for me

Oh thanks for the suggestion
But with the way that I've been feeling
I can't quite think of anything
So completely unappealing

I'd like to go into hiding
For at least a month or two
I'd like to record a voicemail greeting
That really sums up my mood

And like at the end of a bad date
Or a failed interview
It would say, rather simply:

Don't call us. We'll call you.

THAT FIRST YEAR

The year that two became three
No. More. Hot. Tea.

The year of not leaving your side
For more than an hour
And feeling revived
From a two minute shower

The year of white noise
Cuddles and baby slings
As you slowly adjust
To the outside things

The year of sleep regressions
Monkey impressions
Panicked Google searches
Too many to mention

The year I realised that women
Really do hold all the powers
Rocking and pacing
For hours and hours

Being more selective of
The company I keep
And dreading that question
So how does he sleep?

The year of building all the rods
For my own back
Binning the baby books
And not looking back

Endless walks with the pram
To help you to nap
Pounding the pavements
Looking like crap

One whole year to realise
That there's no wrong or right
There's what works
What you *need*
In the middle of the night

The year of doubts and fears
And bending the ears
Of family and friends
He'll sleep eventually
But *when?*

But you're more than
Your sleep struggles
So much more

You're that look of wonder
At a knock on the door

Your giggles
Your protests
And that tiny roar

Beaming with pride
As you take in your stride
Learning to roll
Crawl
And stand
And wave your wee hand

A sudden respect for those
Who've done all this before
But with two
With three
With four
Or more

The year of grand plans and dreams
Of these homemade cuisines
But some days just called
For eggs, chips and beans

And yet somehow you thrived
And we just about survived
The hourly wake-ups
And some almost-breakups

You really did shake-up
These two kids

BABY BORE

Turns out I'm one of
Those mums
An oversharing
Snap-happy-with-a-camera
One

The type I swore I'd never become
Shoot me I said
Well
You'd better get your gun

Oh the old me
Would be most unimpressed
Come on now love
Give it a rest
But first a quick photo
Because I've just got him dressed

See, now I sort of get it
On those really rubbish days
How a flurry of interest
Can colour the grey

That's why I'll always 'like'
That baby pic
Even if his little face
Is proper getting on my wick

Because you don't know
What kind of night she's had
Early morning rows
With the baby's dad
Missing her old life
Really quite bad

Feeling out of place
At baby groups
Toddlers had her
Jumping through hoops
And that like of yours
Could really give her a boost

Oh no! Not another!
I hear you groan
You know this boy's face
Better than your own

You really have seen quite enough
Could spot that kid
In a police lineup
And yes he does look
A bit
Like Donald Trump

But
Better to be kind
Instead of honest
Give them that like
You'll not regret it
I promise

I know this will probably
Make you think twice
The next time I'm so
Loose with my likes

But worry not
I really meant it with yours
The cutest baby on Insta
Of course

SELF-CARE

Self-care
SELF-care

If only I had the inclination
To put into action
All the books
I bought myself
On self-care

They sit upon
That shelf there

Making a mockery of me
And my unwashed hair

The trouble
You see
With self-care
Is *me*

Cos I'm required to do it
Myself

IN PURSUIT OF A NAP

If you ever see a mum
Pacing with a pram nearby
With her head bowed down
Can't quite look you in the eye

Don't boom a loud hello
Or stop her for a chat
Just let her walk on by
She's in pursuit of a nap

The hours that she's wasted
Chasing down this hush
The mileage she's accrued
The pavements that she's trudged

She's becoming quite the pro
The warning signs, she's learned
Any usual suspects
And she'll make a sharp U-turn

A gaggle of giggling teenagers
Blissfully ignorant to her woes
A smartly dressed businessman
About to blow his nose

The murmur of the playground
With the odd erratic scream
A self-service checkout
Talking machines

All these noise-making clowns
Stalling his dreams
Can't they just pipe down?
Don't they know it's almost three?

She was making real progress
She even got a yawn
His eyes were closing over
Until you beeped your bloody horn

ODE TO DUNDEE

Dundee
City by the sea
The place that made
A mother out of me
Gave birth to *The Beano*
And my Casey
Sunniest place in Scotland. Apparently.

You were magic and peaceful
But often lonely
Miles from our family
Just us three

I spent those baby days
In a sleepless haze
Looking out over
The River Tay
Feeling stormy and treacherous
But steady you'd stay

A whole year on your streets
To find my feet
And lose my mind
Repeatedly

Walks with the pram
Religiously
Out. Come rain or shine
Just like 'Fast Eddie'

Singing his tunes
On that corner, near Boots
It's been a hard day's night
He was singing to me
A Dundee treasure, isn't he?

Oh Dundee
You proved to be
The perfect retreat
Fresh air by the sea
Locals easy-going
And judgement-free
With just the right amount
Of friendly

And for that
We'll be
Forever
Yours
Gratefully

MARTYR MOTHER

What did I think?
That I'd go down in history
For giving up myself
So entirely?

Is there some sort of prize
For self-sacrifice?
If there is such a thing
Then it's totally mine

Because I'm a Martyr Mother
A mother like no other
Wearing my exhaustion
Like a badge of honour

A regular Mother Teresa
A full-on people-pleaser
Yeah, Mother Mary
She's got nothing on me

All sense of worth
Turned to dust
I'll serve the bread
But eat the crusts

How about being
Just 'good enough'?
Introducing
A few shortcuts

Like those mums that have
A spring in their step
Whilst I'm over here
Hanging on by a thread

Hair down to my waist
And bare of face
Disappearing from sight
Bowed out of the race

This taking care of me
Whilst looking after you
I just can't seem
To reconcile the two

Because I'm a Martyr Mother
A mother like no other
Wearing my exhaustion
Like a badge of honour

IT'S DIFFERENT NOW

He's off to work
Bearing the weight of the bills
Her indoors
With twelve hours to fill
And up six times in the night, still

Each thinking that the other
Has struck the better deal

Casting up
And putting down
Petty remarks and resentments
Abound
So much more to disagree about now

Negotiating lie-ins
That were once spent together
Taking turns
When one is under the weather

Tag-teaming
Ships in the night
That never-ending
Relay race

Passing the baton
For another hour
Right, it's your turn
I'm off for a shower

But when all's said and done
If I could choose anyone to
Navigate through
This parenthood
It would always
Be you

Eavesdropping and smiling
At the little chats you have
Remembering that actually
You're a bloody good dad

But oh remember
That bloated adolescence of ours?
Carefree and easy
Doing nothing for hours

And of course, I wouldn't change it
It's better now we've him

I guess what I'm saying is
I miss you. A bit

MUM FRIENDS

They're a funny sort-of friend
Not one you'd really choose to meet
Nothing much in common
'Cept these children at your feet

A friendship thrust upon you
In a strange twist of fate
Because you happened to be frisky
Round-about the same date

All rattling around together
In this lost property box
A heap of tired mums
Wearing the same old stripy tops

You'd peruse all your options
But you're running short on time
You've a non-sleeping child?
Well, *you'll* do just fine

They don't care one bit
If your conversation's
Pretty shit
They'll gladly lend an ear
In fact they bloody love it

They'll listen avidly
To your boring
Birth story
That you can never
Quite
Finish
Prop...er...ly

Broken sentences
Snippets
Here and there
(Between nappy changes
And sippy cup exchanges)
But you really don't care
You're just glad to see an adult
Get some fresh air

A person you once referred to
As so-and-so's mum
Will slowly grow upon you
And firm friends
You will become

An ally in this life
Someone to vent
And scream and shout
A sister of sorts
Who you couldn't be without

IN THE TRENCHES

It's funny
I never *got* that expression before
But suddenly I'm here
And I couldn't agree more

Because
I'm up to my neck in it
Fighting my own private war

I've trudged through this motherhood
For everyone to see
Some days I thought I'd had it nailed
Most days it's nailed me

I've dodged
And I've dived
But yeah
I've survived
And I'm stronger than before

I might have lost some battles
But I know
I'll win the war

ALWAYS THE TEETH

He could be having a little grizzle
Or a full on tantrum in the street
One thing is for certain
I will always blame his teeth

I think he's teething
I'll say
Explaining away
The latest ailment
Of the day

I'm inclined to blame his teeth
For all our worldly woes
Those pesky little gnashers
Like to keep us on our toes

So as A-level grades dip
And house values plummet
Stop looking for the culprit
It was Casey's teeth
What done it

GROWING PAINS

You arch your back and cry
At this world unknown to you
All fingers and thumbs
I bring you slowly to my boob

Maybe you're hungry?
Maybe this will do?
It's awkward and I'm clumsy
I'm still getting used to you

You wake each hour at night
Something's really bothering you
Then you break out with big smiles
As you start the day anew

I trudge tiredly to the kitchen
And lament the sleep I knew
I'm not yet loving this
But I'm really trying to

You writhe and groan in pain
At every tooth that's pushing through
I rock and feed and ache
In my attempts to comfort you
It's a game of trial and error
That I'm learning too

You really take some tumbles
When grasping something new
You try
And fail
And try again
I could learn a lot from you

You kick and scream and shout
As you hit the tender twos
I forget what I'm about
And raise my voice at you
Sometimes I get it wrong
Because I'm growing too

ODE TO THE MIGHTY NAP

That little gift for parents
Our child's daytime sleep
A tiny slice of heaven
Where I can lay down in a heap

Or stare blankly at the wall
Just being me

A brief pause
From the day's chores
And mishaps
I've cried over missed naps
No, really
I have

There was a time when
He would only nap on me
Then something changed
And I was suddenly hands-free

Oh, but what to do?
Should I get all the things done?
This could be my only chance
To finally
Get my snack on

Tea, toast, biscuits
That staple mum diet
I'll maybe make a sandwich
Really have a riot

Quick, close the curtains
Keep the world at bay
Telly on
Feet up
Kick the toys out the way

But there's always that niggling feeling
That you'll wake up any minute
I guess that's what makes it sacred
There's a sort of thrill in it

It's been at least an hour now
I'm almost feeling sane
Oh no!
I hear you stirring

Here we go again

JUST STOP IT

Oh so Harry's self-settling
And sleeping through?
You just kiss him
And turn out the light?
Casey still needs boobing
And rocking to sleep
Then is up six times in the night

Is Josh in his big-boy bed yet?
Yes? Wow you must be so proud
Casey's still wearing his Grobags
Should he be using a duvet by now?

And how's Isla with her food these days?
Casey's a real fusspot
He's lost so much weight
With this gastro then flu
And he refuses dinner
A lot

How many words does Oli know now?
Casey says *hi* and *bye*
And everything's *blue*
Apparently, he should know
Over two hundred
By the time he reaches two

How's Luna with brushing her teeth?
Well Casey's an absolute mare
And back teeth? Forget it!
He clamps his mouth shut
There's no way I'm getting back there

What time does Benji go down for his nap?
Do you let him sleep after three?
People say he'd wake less in the night
But I need that time for me

How's Charlie getting on at nursery?
He's coming on leaps and bounds
I worry that Casey gets bored with
Just me
And that he's somehow
Missing out

Just stop it, Mummy
What are you doing?
Don't be silly
I just need you

Your love and your hugs
An occasional dip in the tub
And maybe a biscuit or two

Yes you're so right
I'm missing it all
You're not what you can
And can't do

I'm sorry my love
I got lost in the noise
When I should just enjoy
The unique
And the wonderful
You.

S.A.H.M

So, what do you do?
Me?
Oh I'm *just* a mum

Stay-at-home-mum
Feel-quite-alone-mum
No-right-to-moan-mum

Call-yourself-a-feminist-mum?
Letting-the-side-down-mum
Don't-you-want-to-have-it-all-mum?
Something-just-for-you-mum?
What-exactly-do-you-DO-mum?

Sit-on-the-couch-mum
Got-the-day-off-mum
Daytime-TV-mum
He'd-really-thrive-in-a-nursery-mum
Big-gap-in-your-CV-mum
No-good-for-the-economy-mum

So-what's-for-tea-mum?

THEY SAID

You're spoiling him too much
You'll regret that, they said
They denied us of our rods
And filled our hearts with dread

You're not doing yourself any favours
You should nip that in the bud, they said
Don't you want your evenings back?
You'll never get him out your bed

THEY SAID
THEY SAID
THEY SAID

Sleep training culture
Were you supposed
To *save* our tears?

Because you only added to them
By planting doubts and fears
And by "stealing new parents' joy
For the last one hundred years"[1]

---

1. Quote from Hannah Hackett

But the tide is
Starting to turn now
There's a new voice
On the rise
And we're taking back the role
You had us inconvenienced by

In ourselves we trust
And instinct is our guide
We'll meet them
At their point of need
At this crucial time of life

And *WE SAY*
This is normal
And *WE SAY*
This is fine

Sleepless nights and sacrifice
Are par for the course
Because *Mother* stands for comfort
And I'm so glad to be yours

FIERCELY GENTLE MOTHER

Attachment
Gentle
Crunchy
Intensively motherly

Yeah I suppose
In some ways
That's the mum
I turned out to be

But please don't mistake
Any of these things
For a passive timidity

Don't condemn me as a martyr
To this child that I adore
He who took this rabbit heart of mine
And taught it how to roar

Don't label me a pushover
For meeting his every need
Because I'll fiercely defend the practices
That supposedly make me weak

I'll wake frequently in the night
For as long as he needs

I'll not chase every milestone
But rather follow his lead

I'll recognise when he's struggling
And lashing out at me

I'll not retaliate with punishment
But hold him tenderly

I'll ask if he wants a cuddle
When he's screaming in the street

I'll try to exhibit a kind of patience
That doesn't come so naturally

I'll bend over backwards
With such fierce ferocity

You see
It takes a lot of strength
To be
So very 'weak'

HIDE AND SEEK

Oh Daddy's just great
He's magic alright
A regular Houdini
Disappearing from sight

Alakazam-Alakazoo!
He's especially good
At hiding from you

Just turned around
And he's vanished from view
He's permanently residing
In our downstairs loo

Got all the mod cons
And broadband too

Go find Daddy
Where's Daddy gone?
My not-so-subtle hints
It's been far too long

I'm off like a shot
As soon as he's back
Straight up the stairs
In two seconds flat

And into the shower
For the next few hours
But, let's not be exact

Yes
Two can play
At this disappearing act

LAST MUM STANDING

Everyone's dropping like flies
Round ours
All come down
With hand, foot and mouth

But not Mum
No
She's not allowed

I'm reminded of those endurance shows
Last MAN standing
Hmm
I don't think so

You see her job
Requires a certain physicality
Not to mention
The right mentality
And a bloody-minded tenacity

Yes, you dragged a heavy load
For a couple of miles
But she's pushed that
Through her birth canal

And whilst I don't mean to belittle
Your obstacle course
Did you know that
She's an actual food source?

Let me tell *you* about
Blood, sweat and tears
She's been rocking
Two stone to sleep
For the last two years

She'll take your
Scary Sergeant Major
And raise you
A tantruming threenager

She's pushed to her limits
Every single day
The SAS
Would be a holiday

Because when it comes to real life
She can endure like no other
Look after you all
Handle it
Like a mother.

AWOL

Has anybody seen
The girl I used to be?
We gained a little life
But in the process
We lost me

And only really he
Can truly really see
How motherhood left its mark
Irrevocably

Call off the search
Her bridges have been burned
She just popped out for milk one day
And never returned

She's been replaced by
This knock-off Stepford wife
Whose going through the motions
Living a version of her life

She almost looks the same
A similar sort of height
But something's different about her smile
Something's missing from her eyes

She's lost the sense of silly
That favours the carefree
Bogged down now
With responsibility
Takes every little thing
So seriously

Maybe it's in her makeup
The way that she's wired
She'd report a malfunction
If she wasn't so bloody tired

I wonder where the old one is
I hope that she's alright
Had I known she'd up and leave us
Then I might have said *goodbye*

HELICOPTER MUM

I wish I was an easy, breezy mum
Coffee in hand
Take each moment
As it comes

But me
I'm one of those hovering ones
I flutter and flitter
And ruin your fun

I interfere
Much more than I oughta
I'm a great big bloody helicopter

Providing my running commentary
Gentle hands darling!
Like this, see?

Oh I think that little boy had it first
Why don't we share?
Take it in turns

I'm always there, fearing the worst
Imagined fingers in eyes
And violent outbursts

Awkwardly hovering overhead
I'm right there
Stalking your every step

I know how much cooler
I would be
If I could just quit
My helicopter tendencies

Life surely would be better
If I could relax a bit
Lose the propeller

WHAT A SHAME

You're mum shaming me!
Is all that I see
When someone dares to
To speak up
About what they believe

When did we start to take things
So personally?
Just because
We might do things
Differently

You do you
And I'll do me
And we can coexist
Happily

But can we also share
Our experiences
Without worrying what
The repercussions will be?

And yes
I know we're all
Just 'doing our best'
But let's not
Silence each other
For fear of unrest

And yes
We should word things
Sensitively

But if
I *feel* something
Then, surely
That's on me?

KAMIKAZI KID

Kamikazi Kid
Ruled by your id
On a mission
Most days
To turn mummy grey

Risk taker
Heartbreaker
Mischief-maker
Nerve shaker

Little fingers
In all those hinges
Seeking out means to
Sustain new injuries

Up all night
Not dreaming
But scheming
Of ways to give me a fright

Hot pans and knives
And those bloody great heights
You're really not fussy
Any old platform will suffice

Launching headfirst from
Bookcase
Fireplace
The nearest tree
You're clearly immune to gravity

And wouldn't it be nice
Just once in a while
To look up and not find you
On a 30 spin cycle

Must every single hour
Fill me with dread?
Sit down
On your bottom
Read a book instead

Fearless little person of mine
Who I actually quite like
Shall we just try
Somehow
To keep you alive?

WEANERS

For Natalie Matthews (one of my favourite weaners)

Sometimes to me
Parenting just seems to be
Constantly having to wean
From one bad habit
Onto another

In fact, that's what I'd call us
Weaners not mothers

All these things to pick up
Then suddenly drop
No sooner have you mastered it
They want you to stop

You really should wean him
Off the boob by one
But not a day sooner
Because, y'know, food's just for fun!

Don't you think he's getting
Too big for that dummy?
Dip it in vinegar
Give it to the Easter Bunny

But your utter insistence
That I really should wean
Says much more of you
Than it does of me

Do you think it's something
I should add to my CV?
Additional Skills
Well, did you know I can wean?

Some are so adept
Take it all in their stride
Hit every weaning milestone
Right on time
Like some beautiful,
Gleaming,
Weaning machines

Well, I must be broken
Or missing a bit
Because I'm just so
Bloody rubbish at it

Still on the boob
After two
So many rods
I could open a shop

But who am I weaning him for really?
I'm not sure it's for him
Or even for me
But rather
Some abstract idea
Of the way things *should* be

It's something I worry about
Almost daily
Always there
It's intrusive
And weighs down heavy

So we scramble around
On the internet
Seeking out mums
Who've cracked it

What worked for you?
Will it work for me?
And be honest, tell me
How awful will it be?

He'll scream on the first night
But be fine come night three

I wonder what would happen
If we just let things be
Allow things to happen
More naturally
Not coerce
Or force

But wait
Patiently

THE PARENTAL PARADOX

He's so clingy and needy
And I can't put him down
He only wants me
I'm totally touched out

So I push and I push
And still he won't budge
I know you can do it
You just need a little nudge

Push, push, push
Rush, rush, rush
Come on now my love
We all have to grow up

Always looking ahead
To the next
And the next
Until you're finally left
With that empty nest

And suddenly now
It's me holding on tight
Seperation anxiety
Waking up in the night

Stay with me a while
We don't see you enough
Come on now Mum
We all have to grow up

HAVE A WORD

Somebody better tell
Mrs Lioness
That she's *doing it for herself*
That her cub there is too old now
And her milk has passed its shelf

Ask *her* to be more discreet
I double dare you to
She's flirting with your husband
And showing off too

And Mrs Chimpanzee
Yeah, I wanna be like you!
You nurse there in the open air
Whilst I find the nearest loo

Isn't nature beautiful
But only for a few

Funny how
The mothers
Have more freedom
In a Zoo

MOTHERWHELMED

Off the boob
On the potty
The list has started now

All these things
To cross off
And I'm failing
On all counts

These milestones
Are more like rocks
Weighing me down

In a sea of expectation
So deep
I might just drown

MOTHER OF ALL CONTRADICTIONS

I'm so happy with my choices
Yet question them daily

I've never felt so accomplished
At something I'm failing

I'm excited for the future
Yet always looking back

I'm bursting at the seams
With all the things that I lack

I'm vacant
But always so *full* of you

I've learned so much
But still don't have a clue

I'm close to my limit
But can't get enough

I'm put upon, I'm passive
But undeniably tough

I'm gentle
But can't help shouting

I'm certainly
Doubting

I'm oblivious
But care, so much, what you think

I'm the steady, stable one
Always teetering on the brink

I've never cared for alcohol
But could probably use a drink

I'm unemployed
Yet have never worked so bloody hard

I'm that happy smiling soul
Who's full of mard

I'm permanently skint
But have never felt richer

I'm mindfully looking
At the bigger picture

I need a break
But always want you close

I'm invisible
But have never felt so exposed

I give others advice
I can't seem to follow

I find yours, especially
Hard to swallow

I complain that I'm lonely
But just want to be alone

I'm positively grateful
But love a good moan

I'm absent
Yet ever-present

I'm dull
But effervescent

I'm tired
Yet enlivened

I'm loving this
But can't abide it

I'm strong in my beliefs
Yet lack conviction

I'm reality TV
And a work of fiction

I'm the Mother
Of all contradictions

DADS MATTER TOO

I know you think I never see
All those little things you do
And I know how you hate poetry
But this one's just for you

Your mornings are a long goodbye
With all the warmth that you can find
You're always rushing out the door
Never get to work on time

You gently push him
To try the new
And daring things
I never do

The bigger slides
And scary rides
He has a lot more
Fun with you

You're the best giddy-upper
You're a human climbing frame
He sees you a lot less than me
But he loves you just the same

You do the funniest voices
And all the farmyard noises
Even though you hate to read

You break all the rules
You're much more cool
You're the good cop
Compared to me

And every night
You burst through the door
With arms open wide
Even when
Your day's been shit

Coat off
Bag down
Straight in the lounge
To empty out
The stickle bricks

You carry him around for hours
Just because he's asked you to
You've acquired these sudden biceps
(Yes. I noticed those too)

So, yes
I see all that you are
And all the ways
That he loves you

But I wrote these words
For everyone
Because
Dads matter too

ENJOY EVERY MINUTE

I'm eternally grateful
But occasionally fed up
I can have a little moan
And still love him just as much

I can't imagine my life
Without him in it
But are we really obliged
To 'enjoy every minute'?

Every tantrum
Every wake-up
Every plate of food that's thrown
Sure, I'll lap up all the good stuff
But I think I'll pass on those

Because whilst I'm #blessed
And couldn't be without him
Sometimes this is just hard
And we're allowed to talk about it

BIN DAY

Do you even know
The power that you hold?
Amongst two
And three
And four-year-olds

Yeah the policeman
He's alright
And the postman's pretty zen
But you lot
Well, to Casey
Are neon Gods amongst men

The flashing of your lights
That steady beeping sound
This vehicle is reversing
And Casey's waking now

His eyes are barely open
His hair is all askew
His little legs are racing
To get a better view

The neighbours looking over
Her children all grown now
A happy-sad reminder
Of what made their world go round

The rumbling of the bin wheels
Sets his face aglow
The rubbish has been taken
But where does it go?

It's over in an instant
But his whole day has been made
So, maybe, come next Friday
Give a little wave?

TWO

If you're anything like me
It's quite unlikely
That you'll form a single memory
Before the age of three

But don't worry, Casey
I'll remember for you
All the things
You loved to do
When you were just two

The way you call me 'ma'
Like some cranky
New Yorker
And actively pursue
The bin men
A tiny toddling stalker

A smile and a wave
For everyone you pass
Chasing the dogs
And pointing at cars

Not tarnished yet
By social expectation
I have to laugh
When you walk over
So brazen
Offering up raisins
To those teenage boys

As if to say
Can I play?
So sweet and unfazed
When they look the other way

This past year
You've survived mainly
On macaroni cheese
Sweetcorn and peas
And the odd rich tea
I'm not too sure
How we've dodged scurvy

You're starting to push the limits now
Like any spirited child
Pushing mummy to stop being
So meek
And so mild

You see
Helping you grow has been
Simultaneously
The undoing
But also the making, of me

Little hints now
Of the grown up boy
You'll be
Put your own shoes on
And brush your own teeth
I use the word 'brush' *very* lightly

That look that says
No! Mum, I can do it better
They were right, weren't they?
I don't get to keep you forever

Because now that we've passed
Those testing baby days
And come so far
In so many ways

I'd really quite like it
If you could stay
A little bit longer
This way

Do you think maybe
We could slow down time?
So I could enjoy this
Ragamuffin of mine

Cheeky little face
And messy golden mop
Without that interfering sound
Of the tick-tock

Couldn't we just momentarily
Stall?

Two
It's not so terrible really
At all

VANITY PROJECT

I love how he looks
Simultaneously
Like us both
Your eyes, your smile
But my wonky nose

And doesn't he look like my side
Especially when he cries
All red and blotchy-faced
And bloodshot eyes

I hope he loves music, and art, and film
I hope he's got my rhythm
And your drawing skills

I hope he gets our best traits
Yes, I'd really love that
Your brutal honesty
But my thoughtful tact

How he'll actually turn out
Only time will tell
But I suspect he'll mostly be
Exactly like
Himself.

THE FIRST ACT

I fed you for the last time today
With tears streaming down my face
It almost took my breath away
For, in my mind, a movie played

Starring a thousand little Caseys
Over several different stages
And like every good edit
All the bad parts were erased

A feeling that things
Will never quite be the same
A loss of a closeness
That we'll somehow now reclaim

Because it's not really over
Not nearly, in fact
But merely, the end
Of the first act

END OF AN ERA

Let our little walks into town
Take longer than they should
Let's stop and smell the roses
Take a good, long look

They'll be less tugging
And *'Right, come on then'* from me
Because soon you'll be a brother
And I'll be more busy

Let two books turn into five
Or maybe even ten
How can I deny
'Again, again, again'

Let's snuggle here a little longer
Let the big hand go past three
Let the washing tumble over
Dad can sort his own tea

Let the mess run amok
Whilst we have games to play
Towers to build
And dragons to slay

All these funny little things
Seem so much bigger now
I guess this really means
Time is nearly running out

So I'm soaking up this bit
When it's just me and you
Before my heart explodes
And I'm somehow split in two

And I will love them just as much
And as fiercely as you
And I will tell them it's because
Their brother taught me to

NEXT TIME AROUND

Next time around
I'm leaving Google alone
Ignoring their advice
And heeding my own

I'm rejecting this notion
Of what's 'normal' and 'right'
I'm expecting you
To wake lots in the night

I'm parting ways
With Doubt and Fear
Because they're no longer
Welcome here

I'm stopping the comparisons
With every so-and-so
I'm slaying in my lane
And claiming you as my own

I'm reading these words
And smiling, you know
Because it's not just our babies
That grow

ACKNOWLEDGEMENTS

Thank you to my sister Lauren. These words would never have seen the light of day if it wasn't for you. I am so grateful to you for your encouragement in this and everything else.

A big thank you to Mike for your editing brilliance and commitment to 'scansion'. Not to mention your much-needed policing of exclamation marks! Toodles!

Thank you to my incredibly supportive followers on social media. I have been so encouraged by the lovely messages I've received from you. It has meant more than you might think.

And the biggest thank you, of course, to Casey and Spence; my two best friends and daily source of inspiration. Love you.

ABOUT THE AUTHOR

Karen McMillan lives in Oxfordshire with her partner Spence and her two year-old son Casey.

She penned her first poem 'That First Year' just before Casey's first birthday and the poem became a viral hit.

She continues to share her poetry and thoughts on motherhood under the alias of Mother Truths.

Follow me on:
Instagram: @mother_truths
Facebook: /mymothertruths